DIRTY · LITTLE · LIMERICKS

DIRTY · LITTLE ·

LIMERICKS

AVENEL BOOKS · NEW YORK

AVENEL 1980 EDITION

Manufactured in the United States of America

Library of Congress Cataloging in Publication Data
Main entry under title:

Dirty little limericks.

1. Limericks. 2. Bawdy poetry.
PN6231.L5D54   821'.08'08   80-17671
ISBN: 0-517-320983

p   o   n   m   l

CONTENTS

FOREWORD

A good friend of mine—a practicing therapist—has advanced the thesis that the greatest contribution to human health and sanity in the last two hundred years is neither penicillin nor indoor plumbing, but rather the limerick. He often prescribes limericks for his patients, particularly in cases of depression and melancholy. He also claims that they have a tonic effect on everyone, and does not hesitate to share his enthusiasm. It was through my friend's addiction that I came to study the lure of the limerick.

Limericks first appeared in England around 1820, in a popular party game, in which each participant had to make up a five-line nonsense rhyme. After each extemporaneous recitation, the assembled group sang a chorus ending with the punch line, "Will you come up to Limerick?" Since the parties usually included a certain amount of drinking, the verses tended to get bawdier as the evening wore on. From this sprang the tradition of the dirty little limerick.

Of course, limericks are not exclusively confined to the bawdy. They have been used to express every kind of thought, from the philosophic to principles of physics. Often, limericks are purely nonsensical rhymes, such as those of Edward Lear, whose *Book of Nonsense* (1846) did much to popularize the form. But, because the limerick is a playful, light form, with origins in the people's entertainment, it is perhaps most appropriate when used to portray the foibles and trials of human love.

In most cases, the original authorship of a limerick is unknown. Often the author wished to remain anonymous, if only because his subject matter was hardly suited to polite Victorian parlor conversation. Sometimes the verse seemed to appear spontaneously—on a tavern wall, in a broadside, or as a street urchin's song. Sometimes there were multiple authors, who modified and improved upon preceding efforts, so that the limerick would change subtly with each recitation. In our century, several authorities have made serious efforts to research and collect early limericks, and to discover their authorship where possible. Such serious scholarly study seems to miss an essential aspect of the limerick. The main point of a limerick, after all, is the laugh it draws, not the name of its creator. A limerick is something just for fun, an exercise in cleverness.

The verses selected here have endured because they express a congenial curiosity about people and their affairs. They are bold and explicit, but with a strong element of humor throughout. We hope that the reader will have as much fun in wandering through this collection as the editors did in selecting limericks for it, a difficult chore when one is laughing so hard.

Don't hesitate to play with them yourself—changing words and improvising upon images. The limerick is for everyone, and good for everyone. As my friend would say, take one every few hours as needed. If symptoms persist, increase dosage until smile returns and belly laugh occurs. Continue as desired.

—R. Scott Latham

LITTLE ROMANCES

There was a young lady of Arden,
The tool of whose swain wouldn't harden.
    Said she with a frown,
  " I've been sadly let down
By the tool of a fool in a garden. "

There was a young girl in Berlin
Who was fucked by an elderly Finn.
    Though he diddled his best,
    And fucked her with zest,
She kept asking, " Hey, Pop, is it in ? "

I wooed a stewed nude in Bermuda,
I was lewd, but my God! she was lewder.
    She said it was crude
    To be wooed in the nude—
I pursued her, subdued her, and screwed her!

There was a young lady of Bicester
Who was nicer by far than her sister :
    The sister would giggle
    And wiggle and jiggle,
But this one would come if you kissed her.

There was a young sailor from Brighton
Who remarked to his girl, " You're a tight one. "
    She replied, " 'Pon my soul,
    You're in the wrong hole;
There's plenty of room in the right one. "

A young woman got married at Chester,
Her mother she kissed and she blessed her.
    Says she, " You're in luck,
    He's a stunning good fuck,
For I've had him myself down in Leicester. "

A lady while dining at Crewe
Found an elephant's whang in her stew.
    Said the waiter, " Don't shout,
    And don't wave it about,
Or the others will all want one too. "

There was a young lady of Dover
Whose passion was such that it drove her
    To cry, when you came,
   " Oh dear!   What a shame!
Well, now we shall have to start over. "

➤

There was a young man of Dumfries
Who said to his girl, " If you please,
    It would give me great bliss
    If, while playing with this,
You would pay some attention to these! "

➤

There was a young lady named Flynn
Who thought fornication a sin,
    But when she was tight
    It seemed quite all right,
So everyone filled her with gin.

➤

There was a young fellow named Goody
Who claimed that he wouldn't, but would he?
    If he found himself nude
    With a gal in the mood,
The question's not woody but could he?

There was a young girl from Hong Kong
Who said, " You are utterly wrong
    To say my vagina
    's the largest in China,
Just because of your mean little dong. "

❧

There was once a sad Maître d'hôtel
Who said, " They can all go to hell !
    What they do to my wife—
    Why it ruins my life;
And the worst is, they all do it well. "

❧

There was a young man named Hughes
Who swore off all kinds of booze.
    He said, " When I'm muddled
    My senses get fuddled,
And I pass up too many screws. "

❧

A pansy who lived in Khartoum
Took a lesbian up to his room,
    And they argued all night
    Over who had the right
To do what, and with which, and to whom.

There was an old lady who lay
With her legs wide apart in the hay,
    Then, calling the ploughman,
    She said, " Do it now, man!
Don't wait till your hair has turned gray. "

There was a young plumber of Leigh
Who was plumbing a girl by the sea.
    She said, " Stop your plumbing,
    There's somebody coming! "
Said the plumber, still plumbing, " It's me. "

There was a young fellow from Parma
Who was solemnly screwing his charmer.
    Said the damsel, demure,
    " You'll excuse me, I'm sure,
But I *must* say you fuck like a farmer. "

There was a young man from Purdue
Who was only just learning to screw,
    But he hadn't the knack,
    And he got too far back—
In the right church, but in the wrong pew.

The king named Œdipus Rex
Who started this fuss about sex
    Put the world to great pains
    By the spots and the stains
Which he made on his mother's pubex.

❧

There was a young German named Ringer
Who was screwing an opera singer.
    Said he with a grin,
    " Well, I've sure got it in! "
Said she, " You mean that ain't your finger ? "

❧

A young violinist from Rio
Was seducing a lady named Cleo.
    As she took down her panties
    She said, " No *andantes*;
I want this *allegro con brio!* "

❧

Said a lecherous fellow named Shea,
When his prick wouldn't rise for a lay,
    " You must seize it, and squeeze it,
    And tease it, and please it,
For Rome wasn't built in a day. "

There was a young man from Siam
Who said, " I go in with a wham,
    But I soon lose my starch
    Like the mad month of March,
And the lion comes out like a lamb. "

❧

There was a young fellow named Skinner
Who took a young lady to dinner.
    At a quarter to nine
    They sat down to dine;
At twenty to ten it was in her.
    Skinner?
No, the dinner.

There was a young fellow named Tupper
Who took a young lady to supper.
    At a quarter to nine
    They sat down to dine,
And at twenty to ten it was up her.
    Tupper?
No, Skinner, the son of a bitch!

❧

" My back aches. My penis is sore.
I simply can't fuck any more.
    I'm dripping with sweat,
    And you haven't come yet;
And, my God! it's a quarter to four! "

There was a young lady of Spain
Who took down her pants on a train.
    There was a young porter
    Saw more than he orter,
And asked her to do it again.

❧

There once was a dentist named Stone
Who saw all his patients alone.
    In a fit of depravity
    He filled the wrong cavity,
And my, how his practice has grown!

❧

A sailor who slept in the sun
Woke to find his fly-buttons undone.
    He remarked with a smile,
    " Jesus Christ, a sundial!
And it's now a quarter past one. "

❧

The spouse of a pretty young thing
Came home from the wars in the spring.
    He was lame but he came
    With his dame like a flame—
A discharge is a wonderful thing.

A pretty wife living in Tours
Demanded her daily amour.
    But the husband said, " No!
    It's too much. Let it go!
My backsides are dragging the floor. "

❧

There was a young lady of Twickenham
Who thought men had not enough prick in 'em.
    On her knees every day
    To God she would pray
To lengthen and strengthen and thicken 'em.

❧

A couple was fishing near Clombe
When the maid began looking quite glum,
    And said, " Bother the fish!
    I'd rather coish! "
Which they did—which was why they had come.

❧

The limerick form is complex
Its contents run chiefly to sex.
    It burgeons with virgeons
    And masculine urgeons,
And swarms with erotic effex.

There was a young girl whose frigidity
Approached cataleptic rigidity
    Till you gave her a drink,
    When she quickly would sink
In a state of complaisant liquidity.

ɛ

There was a young fellow named Lancelot
Whom his neighbors all looked on askance a lot.
    Whenever he'd pass
    A presentable lass,
The front of his pants would advance a lot.

ɛ

There was a young student from Yale
Who was getting his first piece of tail.
    He shoved in his pole,
    But in the wrong hole,
And a voice from beneath yelled : " No sale! "

ORGANS

❧

In the Garden of Eden lay Adam,
Complacently stroking his madam,
    And loud was his mirth
    For on all of the earth
There were only two balls—and he had 'em.

❧

A chippy who worked in Black Bluff
Had a pussy as large as a muff.
    It had room for both hands
    And some intimate glands,
And was soft as a little duck's fluff.

❧

There was a young fellow named Bowen
Whose pecker kept growin' and growin'.
    It grew so tremendous,
    So long and so pendulous,
'Twas no good for fuckin'—just showin'.

There was a young lady from Brussels
Who was proud of her vaginal muscles.
    She could easily plex them
    And so interflex them
As to whistle love songs through her bustles.

❧

There was a young girl of Cah'lina,
Had a very capricious vagina :
    To the shock of the fucker
    'Twould suddenly pucker,
And whistle the chorus of " Dinah ."

❧

A lady with features cherubic
Was famed for her area pubic.
    When they asked her its size
    She replied in surprise,
" Are you speaking of square feet, or cubic ? "

❧

There was a young fellow named Cribbs
Whose cock was so big it had ribs.
    They were inches apart,
    And to suck it took art,
While to fuck it took forty-two trips.

There was a young man from Hong Kong
Who had a trifurcated prong :
 A small one for sucking,
 A large one for fucking,
And a *honey* for beating a gong.

   ❧

A fellow whose surname was Hunt
Trained his cock to perform a slick stunt :
 This versatile spout
 Could be turned inside out,
Like a glove, and be used as a cunt.

   ❧

There was a young fellow named Kimble
Whose prick was exceedingly nimble,
 But fragile and slender,
 And dainty and tender,
So he kept it encased in a thimble.

   ❧

There was a young man of Madras
Whose balls were constructed of brass.
 When jangled together
 They played " Stormy Weather, "
And lightning shot out of his ass.

A bad little girl in Madrid,
A most reprehensible kid,
   Told her Tante Louise
   That her cunt smelled like cheese,
And the worst of it was that it did!

❧

There was a young man from Maine
Whose prick was as strong as a cane;
   It was almost as long,
   So he strolled with his dong
Extended in sunshine and rain.

❧

There was a young girl from Medina
Who could completely control her vagina.
   She could twist it around
   Like the cunts that are found
In Japan, Manchukuo and China.

❧

There was a young soldier from Munich
Whose penis hung down past his tunic,
   And their chops girls would lick
   When they thought of his prick,
But alas! he was only a eunuch.

There was a young lady of Natchez
Who chanced to be born with two snatches,
    And she often said, " Shit!
    Why, I'd give either tit
For a man with equipment that matches. "

A girl of uncertain nativity
Had an ass of extreme sensitivity
    When she sat on the lap
    Of a German or Jap,
She could sense Fifth Column activity.

There was a young fellow named Paul
Who confessed, " I have only one ball.
    But the size of my prick
    Is God's dirtiest trick,
For my girls always ask, 'Is that all?' "

A young man from the banks of the Po
Found his cock had elongated so,
    That when he'd pee
    It was not he
But only his neighbors who'd know.

There was a fat man from Rangoon
Whose prick was much like a balloon.
    He tried hard to ride her
    And when finally inside her
She thought she was pregnant too soon.

There was a young lady named Riddle
Who had an untouchable middle.
    She had many friends
    Because of her ends,
Since it isn't the middle you diddle.

There was an old fellow named Skinner
Whose prick, his wife said, had grown thinner.
    But still, by and large,
    It would always discharge
Once he could just get it in her.

There was a young lady from Spain
Whose face was exceedingly plain,
    But her cunt had a pucker
    That made the men fuck her,
Again, and again, and again.

There was a young man from Stamboul
Who boasted so torrid a tool
    That each female crater
    Explored by this satyr
Seemed almost unpleasantly cool.

૏

There was a young fellow of Strensall
Whose pecker was shaped like a pencil,
    Anemic, 'tis true,
    But an interesting screw,
Inasmuch as the tip was prehensile.

૏

A wonderful tribe are the Sweenies,
Renowned for the length of their peenies.
    The hair on their balls
    Sweeps the floors of their halls,
But they don't look at women, the meanies.

૏

There was an old man of Tagore
Whose tool was a yard long or more,
    So he wore the damn thing
    In a surgical sling
To keep it from wiping the floor.

There was a young man of Toulouse
Who had a deficient prepuce,
  But the foreskin he lacked
  He made up in his sac;
The result was, his balls were too loose.

❧

A cautious young fellow named Tunney
Had a whang that was worth any money.
  When eased in half-way,
  The girl's sigh made him say,
" Why the sigh? " " For the rest of it, honey. "

❧

A pious old woman named Tweak
Had taught her vagina to speak.
  It was frequently liable
  To quote from the Bible,
But when fucking—not even a squeak!

❧

When he tried to inject his huge whanger
A young man aroused his girl's anger.
  As they strove in the dark
  She was heard to remark,
" What you need is a zeppelin hangar. "

In the speech of his time, did the Bard
Refer to his prick as his " yard ,"
    But sigh no more, madams :
    ' Twas no longer than Adam's
Or mine, and not one half so hard.

There was a young girl named Dalrymple
Whose sexual equipment was so simple
    That on examination they found
    Little more than a mound
In the center of which was a dimple.

There was a young lady named Grace
Who had eyes in a very odd place.
    She could sit on the hole
    Of a mouse or a mole
And stare the beast square in the face.

The nipples of Sarah Sarong,
When excited, are twelve inches long.
    This embarrassed her lover
    Who was pained to discover
She expected no less of his dong.

A damsel who lives at The Springs
Had her maidenhead ripped into strings
  By a hideous Kurd,
  And now, she averred,
" When the wind blows through it, it sings. "

A Chinaman hailing from Wusih
Once laid an American floozie.
  " How different, " he cried,
  As he slid it inside,
" To diddle a vertical coozie! "

There once was a young man named Lanny
The size of whose prick was uncanny.
  His wife, the poor dear,
  Took it into her ear,
And it came out the hole in her fanny.

There once was an artist named Thayer
Who was really a cubist for fair.
  He looked all his life
  To find him a wife
Possessed of a cunt that was square.

There was a young squaw of Wohunt
Who possessed a collapsible cunt.
  It had many odd uses,
  Produced no papooses,
And fitted both giant and runt.

There was a young laundress named Wrangle
Whose tits tilted up at an angle.
  " They may tickle my chin, "
  She said with a grin,
" But at least they keep out of the mangle. "

STRANGE INTERCOURSE

A young polo-player of Berkeley
Made love to his sweetheart berserkly.
  In the midst of each chukker
  He would break off and fuck her
Horizontally, laterally, and verkeley.

There was a young idler named Blood,
Made a fortune performing at stud,
　　With a fifteen-inch peter,
　　A double-beat metre,
And a load like the Biblical Flood.

There was a young girl of Cape Cod
Who dreamt she'd been buggered by God.
　　But it wasn't Jehovah
　　That turned the girl over,
'Twas Roger the lodger, the sod!

There was a young man in the choir
Whose penis rose higher and higher,
　　Till it reached such a height
　　It was quite out of sight—
But of course you know I'm a liar.

There was a young woman in Dee
Who stayed with each man she did see.
　　When it came to a test
　　She wished to be best,
And practice makes perfect, you see.

There was an old man of Duluth
Whose cock was shot off in his youth.
    He fucked with his nose
    And with fingers and toes,
And he came through a hole in his tooth.

❧

A young man with passions quite gingery
Tore a hole in his sister's best lingerie.
    He slapped her behind
    And made up his mind
To add incest to insult and injury.

❧

There was a young lady named Gloria
Who was had by Sir Gerald Du Maurier,
    And then by six men,
    Sir Gerald again,
And the band at the Waldorf-Astoria.

❧

A newlywed couple from Goshen
Spent their honeymoon sailing the ocean.
    In twenty-eight days
    They got laid eighty ways—
Imagine such fucking devotion!

There was a young fellow named Grimes
Who fucked his girl seventeen times
    In the course of a week—
    And this isn't to speak
Of assorted venereal crimes.

❧

There was a young lady named Hatch
Who would always come through in a scratch.
    If a guy wouldn't neck her,
    She'd grab up his pecker
And shove the damn thing up her snatch.

❧

There was a young lady named Hilda
Who went for a walk with a builder.
    He knew that he could,
    And he should, and he would—
And he did—and he goddam near killed her!

❧

If you're speaking of actions immoral
Then how about giving the laurel
    To doughty Queen Esther,
    No three men could best her—
One fore, and one aft, and one oral.

There was a young fellow of Kent
Whose prick was so long that it bent,
    So to save himself trouble
    He put it in double,
And instead of coming he went.

❧

There was a young man of Kildare
Who was fucking a girl on the stair.
    The bannister broke,
    But he doubled his stroke
And finished her off in mid-air.

❧

There was a young girl from New York
Who plugged up her cunt with a cork.
    A woodpecker or two
    Made the grade, it is true,
But it totally baffled the stork.

Till along came a man who presented
A tool that was strangely indented.
    With a dizzying twirl
    He punctured that girl,
And thus was the cork-screw invented.

There was a young Scot in Madrid
Who got fifty-five fucks for a quid.
　　　When they said, " Are you faint? "
　　　He replied, " No, I ain't,
But I *don't* feel as good as I did. "

❧

A remarkable race are the Persians,
They have such peculiar diversions.
　　　They screw the whole day
　　　In the regular way,
And save up the nights for perversions.

❧

There was a young girl of Rangoon
Who was blocked by the Man in the Moon.
　　　" Well, it *has* been great fun, "
　　　She remarked when he'd done,
" But I'm sorry you came quite so soon. "

❧

There was a young lady named Ransom
Who was rogered three times in a hansom.
　　　When she cried out for more
　　　A voice from the floor
Said, " My name is Simpson, not Samson. "

" Last night, " said a lassie named Ruth,
" In a long-distance telephone booth,
    I enjoyed the perfection
    Of an ideal connection—
I was screwed, if you must know the truth."

There once was a handsome young seaman
Who with ladies was really a demon.
    In peace or in war,
    At sea or on shore,
He could certainly dish out the semen.

There was a young lady from Sydney
Who could take it right up to her kidney.
    But a man from Quebec
    Shoved it up to her neck.
He had a long one, now didn' he?

There was a young man of Tibet,
And this is the strangest one yet—
    His prick was so long,
    And so pointed and strong,
He could bugger six Greeks *en brochette*.

There was a young person of Kent
Who was famous wherever he went.
    All the way through a fuck
    He would quack like a duck,
And he crowed like a cock when he spent.

A zoologist's daughter in Ewing
Gave birth to a bottle of bluing.
    Her father said, " Flo,
    What I want to know
Isn't *whether,* but *what* you've been screwing. "

There was a young lady of Norway
Who hung by her heels in a doorway.
    She said to her beau,
    " Look at me, Joe,
I think I've discovered one more way. "

ORAL IRREGULARITY

There once was a lady from Arden
Who sucked off a man in a garden.
  He said, " My dear Flo,
  Where does all that stuff go ? "
And she said, " (*swallow hard*)—I beg pardon ? "

There was a young girl in Berlin
Who eked out a living through sin.
  She didn't mind fucking,
  But much preferred sucking,
And she'd wipe off the pricks on her chin.

There was a young bride, a Canuck,
Told her husband, " Let's do more than suck.
  You say that I, maybe,
  Can have my first baby—
Let's give up this Frenching, and fuck ! "

King Louis gave a lesson in Class,
One time he was sexing a lass.
    When she used the word " Damn "
    He rebuked her : " Please ma'am,
Keep a more civil tongue in my ass. "

&

There was an old man of Decatur,
Took out his red-hot pertater.
    He tried at her dent
    But when his thing bent,
He got down on his knees and he ate 'er.

&

That naughty old Sappho of Greece
Said, " What I prefer to a piece
    Is to have my pudenda
    Rubbed hard by the enda
The little pink nose of my niece. "

&

A canny Scotch lass named McFargle,
Without coaxing and such argy-bargle,
    Would suck a man's pud
    Just as hard as she could,
And she saved up the sperm for a gargle.

There was a young fellow named Meek
Who invented a lingual technique.
    It drove women frantic
    And made them romantic,
And wore all the hair off his cheek.

❧

There was a young man of Nantucket
Whose prick was so long he could suck it.
    He said with a grin,
    As he wiped off his chin,
" If my ear were a cunt I could fuck it. "

❧

There was a young fellow named Pell
Who didn't like cunt very well.
    He would finger and fuck one,
    But never would suck one—
He just couldn't get used to the smell.

❧

A young bride was once heard to say,
" Oh dear, I am wearing away!
    The insides of my thighs
    Look just like mince pies,
For my husband won't shave every day. "

A worried young man from Stamboul
Discovered red spots on his tool.
    Said the doctor, a cynic,
    " Get out of my clinic!
Just wipe off the lipstick, you fool. "

&

A tidy young lady of Streator
Dearly loved to nibble a peter.
    She always would say,
    " I prefer it this way.
I think it is very much neater. "

&

There was a young girl, very sweet,
Who thought sailors' meat quite a treat.
    When she sat on their lap
    She unbuttoned their flap,
And always had plenty to eat.

&

There was a young fellow named Tucker
Who, instructing a novice cock-sucker,
    Said, " Don't bow out your lips
    Like an elephant's hips,
The boys like it best when they pucker. "

BUGGERY

❦

There was a young man of Arras
Who stretched himself out on the grass,
    And with no little trouble
    He bent himself double
And stuck his prick well up his ass.

❦

Coitus upon a cadaver
Is the ultimate way you can have 'er.
    Her inanimate state
    Means a man needn't wait,
And eliminates all the palaver.

❦

There was a young fellow named Dave
Who kept a dead whore in a cave.
    He said, " I admit
    I'm a bit of a shit,
But think of the money I save! "

An earnest young woman in Thrace
Said, " Darling, that's not the right place! "
    So he gave her a thwack,
    And did on her back
What he couldn't have done face to face.

❧

There was a young lady who said,
As her bridegroom got into the bed,
    " I'm tired of this stunt
    That they do with one's cunt,
You can get up my bottom instead. "

❧

ABUSES OF THE CLERGY

❧

There were three young ladies of Birmingham,
And this is the scandal concerning 'em.
    They lifted the frock
    And tickled the cock
Of the Bishop engaged in confirming 'em.

There was an old abbess quite shocked
To find nuns where the candles were locked.
    Said the abbess, " You nuns
    Should behave more like guns,
And never go off till you're cocked. "

There was a young monk from Siberia
Whose morals were very inferior.
    He did to a nun
    What he shouldn't have done,
And now she's a Mother Superior.

ZOOPHILY

There once was a fellow named Siegel
Who attempted to bugger a beagle,
    But the mettlesome bitch
    Turned and said with a twitch,
" It's fun, but you know it's illegal. "

There was a young girl from Decatur
Who was fucked by an old alligator.
    No one ever knew
    How she relished that screw,
For after he fucked her, he ate her.

❧

EXCREMENT

❧

There was a young man of Rangoon
Who farted and filled a balloon.
    The balloon went so high
    That it stuck in the sky,
And stank out the Man in the Moon.

❧

There was an old lady from Wheeling
Who had a peculiar feeling,
    She laid on her back
    And opened her crack
And pissed all over the ceiling.

GOURMANDS

There was a young fellow named Fritz
Who planted an acre of tits.
    They came up in the fall,
    Pink nipples and all,
And he chewed them all up into bits.

VIRGINITY

There was a young girl named Anheuser
Who said that no man could surprise her.
    But Pabst took a chance,
    Found Schlitz in her pants,
And now she is sadder Budweiser.

There was a young Miss from Cape Cod
Who at soldiers would not even nod.
 But she tripped in a ditch
 And some son-of-a-bitch
Of a corporal raped her, by God!

   ❧

A Salvation Lassie named Claire
Was having her first love affair.
 As she climbed into bed
 She reverently said,
"I wish to be opened with prayer."

   ❧

A girl named Alice, in Dallas,
Had never felt of a phallus.
 She remained virgo intacto,
 Because, ipso facto,
No phallus in Dallas fit Alice.

   ❧

There was a young girl of East Lynne
Whose mother, to save her from sin,
 Had filled up her crack
 To the brim with shellac,
But the boys picked it out with a pin.

There was a young fellow named Fyfe
Who married the pride of his life,
    But imagine his pain
    When he struggled in vain,
And just couldn't get into his wife.

There was a young fellow named Gluck
Who found himself shit out of luck.
    Though he petted and wooed,
    When he tried to get screwed
He found virgins just don't give a fuck.

There was a young girl named McKnight
Who got drunk with her boy-friend one night.
    She came to in bed
    With a split maidenhead—
That's the last time she ever was tight.

There was a young girl from Sofia
Who succumbed to her lover's desire.
    She said, " It's a sin,
    But now that it's in,
Could you shove it a few inches higher ? "

There was a young fellow named Sweeney
Whose girl was a terrible meanie.
    The hatch of her snatch
    Had a catch that would latch—
She could only be screwed by Houdini.

A skinny old maid from Verdun
Wed a short-peckered son-of-a-gun.
    She said, " I don't care
    If there isn't much there.
God knows it is better than none. "

There was a young lady called Wylde,
Who kept herself quite undefiled
    By thinking of Jesus,
    Contagious diseases,
And the bother of having a child.

MOTHERHOOD

❧

There once was a Vassar B.A.
Who pondered the problem all day
    Of what there would be
    If C-U-N-T
Were divided by C-O-C-K.

A young Ph.D. passing by,
She gave him the problem to try.
    He worked the division
    With perfect precision,
And the answer was B-A-B-Y.

❧

There was a young girl who begat
Three brats, by name Nat, Pat, and Tat.
    It was fun in the breeding
    But hell in the feeding,
When she found there was no tit for Tat.

There was a young pessimist, Grotton,
Who wished he had ne'er been begotten,
Nor would he have been
But the rubber was thin,
And right at the tip it was rotten.

There was a young lady named Flo
Whose lover had pulled out too slow.
So they tried it all night
Till he got it just right...
Well, practice makes pregnant, you know.

There was a young lady from Thrace
Whose corsets got too tight to lace.
Her mother said, " Nelly,
There's things in your belly
That never got in through your face. "

There was a young lady named Myrtle
Whose womb was exceedingly fertile.
Her pa got contortions
At all her abortions,
And bought her a chastity girdle.

There was a young girl from Penzance
Who decided to take just one chance.
     So she let herself go
     In the lap of her beau,
And now all her sisters are aunts.

❧

There was a young lady named Sue
Who preferred a stiff drink to a screw.
     But one leads to the other,
     And now she's a mother—
Let this be a lesson to *you*.

❧

There was a young lady of Wantage
Of whom the Town Clerk took advantage.
     Said the County Surveyor,
   " Of course you must pay her;
You've altered the line of her frontage. "

❧

There was a young lady of Maine
Who declared she'd a man on the brain.
     But you knew from the view
     Of the way her waist grew,
It was not on her brain that he'd lain.

PROSTITUTION

꙳

There once was a floozie named Annie
Whose prices were cosy—but canny:
    A buck for a fuck,
    Fifty cents for a suck,
And a dime for a feel of her fanny.

꙳

Said an elderly whore named Arlene,
" I prefer a young lad of eighteen.
    There's more cream in his larder,
    And his pecker gets harder,
And he fucks in a manner obscene. "

꙳

There was a young lady from Cue
Who filled her vagina with glue.
    She said with a grin,
    " If they pay to get in,
They'll pay to get out of it too. "

There was a young girl named Dale
Who put up her ass for sale.
    For the sum of two bits
    You could tickle her tits,
But a buck would get you real tail.

Ș

There was a young girl from Des Moines
Who had a large sack full of coins.
    The nickels and dimes
    She got from the times
That she cradled the boys in her loins.

Ș

A notorious whore named Miss Hearst
In the weakness of men is well versed.
    Reads a sign o'er the head
    Of her well-rumpled bed :
" The customer always comes first. "

Ș

There was an old girl of Kilkenny
Whose usual charge was a penny.
    For the half of that sum
    You could finger her bum—
A source of amusement to many.

Said a madam named Mamie La Farge
To a sailor just off of a barge,
    " We have one girl that's dead,
        With a hole in her head—
Of course there's a slight extra charge. "

&

In the city of York there's a lass
Who will hitch up her dress when you pass.
    If you toss her two bits
        She will strip to the tits,
And let you explore her bare ass.

&

A harlot of note named Le Dux
Would always charge seventy bucks.
    But for that she would suck you,
        And wink-off and fuck you—
The whole thing was simply de luxe!

&

There was a young whore from Madrid
Who anyone could fuck for a quid.
    But a bastard Italian
        With balls like a stallion
Said he'd do it for nothing—and did.

Unique is a strumpet of Mazur
In the way that her clientèle pays her :
    A machine that she uses
    Clamps on to her whoosis,
And clocks everybody that lays her.

There was an old whore named McGee
Who was just the right sort for a spree.
    She said, " For a fuck
    I charge half a buck,
And I throw in the ass-hole for free. "

Said a dainty young whore named Miss Meggs,
" The men like to spread my two legs,
    Then slip in between,
    If you know what I mean,
And leave me the white of their eggs. "

Said Clark Gable, picking his nose,
" I get more than the public suppose.
    Take the Hollywood way,
    It's the women who pay,
And the men simply take off their clothes. "

There was a young lady in Reno
Who lost all her dough playing keeno.
    But she lay on her back
    And opened her crack,
And now she owns the casino.

❖

DuPont, I. G., Monsanto, and Shell
Built a world-circling pussy cartel,
    And by planned obsolescence
    So controlled detumescence
A poor man could not get a smell.

❖

There was a hot girl from the Saar
Who fucked all, both from near and from far.
    When asked to explain,
    She replied with disdain,
"I'm trying to buy me a car."

❖

There was a young girl from St. Cyr
Whose reflex reactions were queer.
    Her escort said, "Mable,
    Get up off the table;
That money's to pay for the beer."

A licentious old justice of Salem
Used to catch all the harlots and jail 'em.
    But instead of a fine
    He would stand them in line,
With his common-law tool to impale 'em.

      ❧

Ethnologists up with the Sioux
Wired home for two punts, one canoe.
    The answer next day
    Said, " Girls on the way,
But what the hell's a 'panoe'? "

      ❧

There was an old Count of Swoboda
Who would not pay a whore what he owed her.
    So with great *savoir-faire*
    She stood on a chair,
And pissed in his whiskey-and-soda.

      ❧

There was an old man of Tagore
Who tried out his cook as a whore
    He used Bridget's twidget
    To fidget his digit,
And now she won't cook any more.

A young girl who was no good at tennis,
But at swimming was really a menace,
　　Took pains to explain,
　"It depends how you train :
I was a street-walker in Venice. "

There once was a harlot at Yale
With her price-list tattooed on her tail,
　　And on her behind,
　　For the sake of the blind,
She had it embroidered in Braille.

The chief charm of a whore in Shalott
Was the absence of hair on her twat.
　　She kept it smooth-looking
　　Not by shaving or plucking,
But by all of the fucking she got.

DISEASES

A sultan named Abou ben Adhem
Thus cautioned a travelling madam,
  " I suffer from crabs
  As do most us A-rabs, "
" It's alright, " said the madam, " I've had 'em. "

There was a young woman of Chester
Who said to the man who undressed her,
  " I think you will find
  That it's better behind—
The front is beginning to fester. "

There was a young rounder named Fisk
Whose method of screwing was brisk.
  And his reason was : " If
  The damned bitch has the syph,
This way I'm reducing the risk. "

There was a young lady named Hitchin
Who was scratching her crotch in the kitchen.
　　Her mother said, " Rose,
　　It's the crabs, I suppose. "
She said, " Yes, and the buggers are itchin'. "

❧

There was a young maid of Klepper
Went out one night with a stepper,
　　And now in dismay
　　She murmurs each day,
" His pee-pee was made of red-pepper! "

❧

A charming young lady named Randall
Has a clap that the doctors can't handle.
　　So this lovely, lorn floozie,
　　With her poor, damaged coosie,
Must take her delight with a candle.

❧

There was a young lady at sea
Who said, " God, how it hurts me to pee. "
　　" I see, " said the mate,
　　" That accounts for the state
Of the captain, the purser, and me. "

A fellow who slept with a whore
Used a safe, but his pecker got sore.
    Said he with chagrin,
  " Selling these is a sin. "
Said the druggist, " *Caveat emptor.* "

❧

There once was a writer named Twain
Who had a peculiar stain
    Surrounding the head
    Of his prick : it was red,
And was said to wash off in the rain.

❧

LOSSES

❧

There was a young sailor named Bates
Who did the fandango on skates.
    He fell on his cutlass
    Which rendered him nutless
And practically useless on dates.

There was a young fellow from Boston
Who rode around in an Austin.
    There was room for his ass
    And a gallon of gas,
But his balls hung outside, and he lost 'em.

There was a young man of Canute
Who was troubled by warts on his root.
    He put acid on these,
    And now, when he pees,
He can finger his root like a flute.

There was a young girl in a cast
Who had an unsavory past,
    For the neighborhood pastor
    Tried fucking through plaster,
And his very first fuck was his last.

There was a young lady of Clewer
Who was riding a bike, and it threw her.
    A man saw her there
    With her legs in the air,
And seized the occasion to screw her.

There was a young lady named Duff
With a lovely, luxuriant muff.
    In his haste to get in her
    One eager beginner
Lost both of his balls in the rough.

➣

And then there's a story that's fraught
With disaster—of balls that got caught,
    When a chap took a crap
    In the woods, and a trap
Underneath... Oh, I can't bear the thought!

➣

There was a young man from Glenchasm
Who had a tremendous orgasm.
    In the midst of his thralls
    He burst both his balls
And covered an acre with plasm.

➣

There was a young man in Havana,
Fucked a girl on a player piano.
    At the height of their fever
    Her ass hit the lever—
Yes! He has no banana!

There was a young man with a hernia
Who said to his surgeon, " Gol-dernya,
   When carving my middle
   Be sure you don't fiddle
With matters that do not concernya. "

❧

There was a young couple named Kelly
Who had to live belly to belly,
   Because once, in their haste,
   They used library paste
Instead of petroleum jelly.

❧

There was a young man of Khartoum
Who lured a poor girl to her doom.
   He not only fucked her,
   But buggered and sucked her—
And left her to pay for the room.

❧

Did you hear about young Henry Lockett?
He was blown down the street by a rocket.
   The force of the blast
   Blew his balls up his ass,
And his pecker was found in his pocket.

There was a young man of Madras
Who was fucking a girl in the grass,
    But the tropical sun
    Spoiled half of his fun
By singeing the hair off his ass.

❧

There was a young man of Missouri
Who fucked with a terrible fury,
    Till hauled into court
    For his besti-al sport,
And condemned by a poorly-hung jury.

❧

All winter the eunuch from Munich
Went walking in naught but a tunic.
    Folks said, " You've a cough;
    You'll freeze your balls off! "
Said he, " That's why I'm a eunuch. "

❧

There was a young lady named Nance
Whose lover had St. Vitus dance.
    When she dove for his prick,
    He wriggled so quick,
She bit a piece out of his pants.

There was an old man from New York
Whose tool was as dry as a cork.
 While attempting to screw
 He split it in two,
And now his tool is a fork.

❧

One evening a workman named Rawls
Fell asleep in his old overalls.
 And when he woke up he
 Discovered a puppy
Had bitten off both of his balls.

❧

A horny young fellow named Redge
Was jerking off under a hedge.
 The gardener drew near
 With a huge pruning shear,
And trimmed off the edge of his wedge.

❧

When the White Man attempted to rule
The Indians made him a fool.
 They cut off his nuts
 To hang in their huts,
And stuffed up his mouth with his tool.

There was a young singer named Springer,
Got his testicles caught in the wringer.
    He hollered with pain
    As they rolled down the drain,
(*falsetto*) : " There goes my career as a singer! "

❧

There was an old rake from Stamboul
Felt his ardor grow suddenly cool.
    No lack of affection
    Reduced his erection—
But his zipper got caught in his tool.

❧

There was a young girl of high station
Who ruined her fine reputation
    When she said she'd the pox
    From sucking on cocks—
She should really have called it " fellation. "

❧

I'd rather have fingers than toes,
I'd rather have ears than a nose,
    And a happy erection
    Brought just to perfection
Makes me terribly sad when it goes.

There was a young lady of Wheeling
Who professed to lack sexual feeling.
But a cynic named Boris
Just touched her clitoris,
And she had to be scraped off the ceiling.

SEX SUBSTITUTES

A man in the battle of Aix
Had one nut and his cock shot away,
But found out in this pickle
His nose could still tickle,
Though he might get the snuffles some day.

A man in the battle of Aix

Nymphomaniacal Alice
Used a dynamite stick for a phallus.
They found her vagina
In North Carolina,
And her ass-hole in Buckingham Palace.

A lesbian lassie named Anny
Desired to appear much more manny.
  So she whittled a pud
  Of mahogany wood,
And let it protrude from her cranny.

A nudist resort at Benares
Took a midget in all unawares.
  But he made members weep
  For he just couldn't keep
His nose out of private affairs.

A squeamish young fellow named Brand
Thought caressing his penis was grand,
  But he viewed with distaste
  The gelatinous paste
That it left in the palm of his hand.

There was a young woman of Croft
Who played with herself in a loft,
  Having reasoned that candles
  Could never cause scandals,
Besides which they did not go soft.

There was a young man from Darjeeling
Whose dong reached up to the ceiling.
    In the electric light socket
    He'd put it and rock it—
Oh God! What a wonderful feeling!

     ❧

A certain young fellow named Dick
Liked to feel a girl's hand on his prick.
    He taught them to fool
    With his rigid old tool
Till the cream shot out, white and thick.

     ❧

An agreeable girl named Miss Doves
Likes to jack off the young men she loves.
    She will use her bare fist
    If the fellows insist
But she really prefers to wear gloves.

     ❧

A fair-haired young damsel named Grace
Thought it very, very foolish to place
    Her hand on your cock
    When it turned hard as rock,
For fear it would explode in her face.

There was a young parson of Harwich,
Tried to grind his betrothed in a carriage.
 She said, " No, you young goose,
 Just try self-abuse.
And the other we'll try after marriage. "

❧

A neurotic young man of Kildare
Drilled a hole in the seat of a chair.
 He fucked it all night,
 Then died of the fright
That maybe he wasn't " all there. "

❧

She made a thing of soft leather,
And topped off the end with a feather.
 When she poked it inside her
 She took off like a glider,
And gave up her lover forever.

❧

A thrifty old man named McEwen
Inquired, " Why be bothered with screwing ?
 It's safer and cleaner
 To finger your wiener,
And besides you can see what you're doing. "

A lusty young woodsman of Maine
For years with no woman had lain,
    But he found sublimation
    At a high elevation
In the crotch of a pine—God, the pain!

There was a young lady named Mandel
Who caused quite a neighborhood scandal
    By coming out bare
    On the main village square
And frigging herself with a candle.

There was a young girl of Mobile
Whose hymen was made of chilled steel.
    To give her a thrill
    Took a rotary drill
Or a Number 9 emery wheel.

There was a young man from Montrose
Who could diddle himself with his toes.
    He did it so neat
    He fell in love with his feet,
And christened them Myrtle and Rose.

There was a young lady from Munich
Who was had in a park by a eunuch.
    In a moment of passion
    He shot her a ration
From a squirt-gun concealed 'neath his tunic.

❧

There was a young man in Norway,
Tried to jerk himself off in a sleigh,
    But the air was so frigid
    It froze his balls rigid,
And all he could come was frappé.

❧

A bobby of Nottingham Junction
Whose organ had long ceased to function
    Deceived his good wife
    For the rest of her life
With the aid of his constable's truncheon.

❧

There was a young fellow named Perkin
Who always was jerkin' his gherkin.
    His wife said, " Now, Perkin,
    Stop jerkin' your gherkin;
You're shirkin' your ferkin'—you bastard! "

There was a young man named Pete
Who was a bit indiscreet.
    He pulled on his dong
    Till it grew very long
And actually dragged in the street.

There was a young man from Racine
Who invented a fucking machine.
    Concave or convex
    It would fit either sex,
With attachments for those in between.

There was a young girl named Miss Randall
Who thought it beneath her to handle
    A young fellow's pole,
    So instead, her hot hole
She contented by means of a candle.

There was a young lady named Rose
Who'd occasionally straddle a hose,
    And parade about, squirting
    And spouting and spurting,
Pretending she pissed like her beaux.

There was a young lady named Rose,
With erogenous zones in her toes.
 She remained onanistic
 Till a foot-fetichistic
Young man became one of her beaux.

❧

There once was a eunuch of Roylem,
Took two eggs to the cook and said, "Boil 'em.
 I'll sling 'em beneath
 My inadequate sheath,
And slip into the harem and foil 'em. "

❧

There's a pretty young lady named Sark,
Afraid to get laid in the dark,
 But she's often manhandled
 By the light of a candle
In the bushes of Gramercy Park.

❧

A milkmaid there was, with a stutter,
Who was lonely and wanted a futter.
 She had nowhere to turn,
 So she diddled a churn,
And managed to come with the butter.

There was a young fellow named Veach
Who fell fast asleep on the beach.
   His dreams of nude women
   Had his proud organ brimming
And squirting on all within reach.

⟫

There was a young fellow from Yale
Whose face was exceedingly pale.
   He spent his vacation
   In self-masturbation
Because of the high price of tail.

⟫

There was a young man from Winsocket
Who put a girl's hand in his pocket.
   Her delicate touch
   Thrilled his pecker so much,
It shot off in the air like a rocket.

ASSORTED ECCENTRICITIES

❧

Floating idly one day through the air
A circus performer named Blair
    Tied a sizeable rock
    To the end of his cock
And shattered a balcony chair.

❧

There was a young man of Australia
Who painted his ass like a dahlia.
    The drawing was fine,
    The color divine,
The scent—ah, that was a failure.

❧

The Reverend Henry Ward Beecher
Called a girl a most elegant creature.
    So she laid on her back
    And, exposing her crack,
Said, " Fuck *that*, you old Sunday School Teacher! "

There was a young man of Belgravia
Who cared neither for God nor his Saviour.
    He walked down the Strand
    With his prick in his hand
And was jailed for indecent behavior.

‽

A vigorous fellow named Bert
Was attracted by every new skirt.
    Oh, it wasn't their minds
    But their rounded behinds
That excited this loveable flirt.

‽

A lazy, fat fellow named Betts
Upon his fat ass mostly sets.
    Along comes a gal
    And says, " *I'll* fuck you, pal. "
Says he, " If you'll do the work, let's. "

‽

There was a young fellow named Bliss
Whose sex life was strangely amiss,
    For even with Venus
    His recalcitrant penis
Would never do better than t
                            h
                            i
                            s
                            .

There once was an actress of Bonely,
And the men never let her be lonely.
    So she hung out in front
    Of her popular cunt
A sign reading : " Standing Room Only. "

There was a gay Countess of Bray,
And you may think it odd when I say,
    That in spite of high station,
    Rank and education,
She always spelt Cunt with a K.

There was a young lady named Bruce
Who captured her man by a ruse :
    She filled up her fuselage
    With a good grade of mucilage,
And he never could pry himself loose.

There was a young fellow named Chick
Who fancied himself rather slick.
    He went to a ball
    Dressed in nothing at all
But a big velvet bow round his prick.

There was a young lady from China
Who mistook for her mouth her vagina.
        Her clitoris huge
        She covered with rouge
And lipsticked her labia minor.

&

An ignorant maiden named Crewe-Pitt
Did something amazingly stupid :
        When her lover had spent
        She douched with cement,
And gave birth to a statue of Cupid.

&

There was a young man of Datchet
Who cut off his prick with a hatchet.
        Then very politely
        He sent it to Whitely,
And ordered a cunt that would match it.

&

There was a young fellow named Dick
Who perfected a wonderful trick :
        With a safe for protection
        He'd get an erection,
And then balance himself on his prick.

A psychoneurotic fanatic
Said, " I take little girls to the attic,
    Then whistle a tune
    'Bout the cow and the moon—
When the cow jumps, I come. It's dramatic. "

        ❧

There was an old fellow named Fletcher,
A lewd and perverted old lecher.
    In a spirit of meanness
    He cut off his penis,
And now he regrets it, I betcha.

        ❧

Said Einstein, " I have an equation
Which science might call Rabelaisian.
    Let P be virginity
    Approaching infinity,
And U be a constant, persuasion.

" Now if P over U be inverted
    And the square root of U be inserted
        X times over P,
        The result, Q.E.D.
Is a relative, " Einstein asserted.

There was a young girlie named Hannah
Who loved madly her lover's banana.
    She loved pubic hair
    And balls that were bare,
And she jacked him off in her bandanna.

❧

A sensitive fellow named Harry
Thought sex too revolting to marry.
    So he went out in curls
    And frowned on the girls,
And he got to be known as a fairy.

❧

There was an announcer named Herschel
Whose habits became controversial,
    Because when out wooing
    Whatever he was doing
At ten he'd insert his commercial.

❧

There was a young lady named Hicks
Who delighted to play with men's pricks,
    Which she would embellish
    With evident relish,
And make them stand up and do tricks.

There was a young girl from Hong Kong
Whose cervical cap was a gong.
    She said with a yell,
    As a shot rang the bell,
" I'll give you a ding for a dong. "

    ❧

There was a young man in Hong Kong
Who grew seven fathoms of prong.
    It looked, when erect,
    About as you'd expect—
When coiled it did not seem so long.

    ❧

That horny old rascal, Manet,
While buggering a boy on the Quay,
    Was attacked by a crick
    In the tip of his prick—
" *Merde!* " he cried, " Quick! Baume Bengué! "

    ❧

Regardez-vous Toulouse-Lautrec,
Though at first glance an ambulant wreck,
    He could fuck once a week
    A la manière antique,
And once in a while *à la Grecque.*

Van Gogh found a whore who would lay,
And accept a small painting as pay.
    " *Vive l'Art!* " cried Van Gogh,
    " But it's too fucking slow—
I wish I could paint ten a day! "

For sculpture that's really first class
You need form, composition, and mass.
    To do a good Venus
    Just leave off the penis,
And concentrate all on the ass.

A young man who lived in Khartoum
Was exceedingly fond of the womb.
    He thought nothing finer
    Than the human vagina,
So he kept three or four in his room.

The last time I dined with the King
He did quite a curious thing :
    He sat on a stool
    And took out his tool,
And said, " If I play, will you sing? "

There was a young lady named Knox
Who kept a pet snake in her box.
    It was trained not to hiss
    When she sat down to piss,
But would nibble the noggins off cocks.

There was a young laundress of Lamas
Who invented high amorous dramas
    For the spots she espied
    Dried and hardened inside
The pants of the parson's pajamas.

There once was a spinsterish lass
Who constructed her panties of brass.
    When asked, " Do they chafe ? "
    She said, " Yes, but I'm safe
Against pinches, and pins in the ass. "

There once was a girl named Louise
Whose cunt-hair hung down to her knees.
    The crabs in her twat
    Tied the hair in a knot,
And constructed a flying trapeze.

The team of Tom and Louise
Do an act in the nude on their knees.
      They crawl down the aisle
      While fucking dog-style,
And the orchestra plays Kilmer's " Trees. "

🙚

Have you heard about Magda Lupescu,
Who came to Rumania's rescue?
      It's a wonderful thing
      To be under a king—
Is democracy better, I esk you?

🙚

A golfer named Sandy MacFarr
Went to bed with a Hollywood star
      When he first saw her gash he
      Cried, " Quick, goot muh mashie !
Uh thunk uh c'n muk it in par. "

🙚

A bus-man named Abner McFuss
Liked to suck off small boys on his bus,
      Then go out and sniff turds
      And the assholes of birds—
He sure was a funny old cuss.

There was a young man from Mobile
Who wondered just how it would feel
    To carry a gong
    Hanging down from his dong,
And occasionally let the thing peal.

So he rigged up a clever device,
And tried the thing out once or twice,
    But it wasn't the gong
    But rather his prong
That peeled, and it didn't feel nice!

There was a young girl of Moline
Whose fucking was sweet and obscene.
    She would work on a prick
    With every known trick,
And finish by winking it clean.

There was a young farmer of Nant
Whose conduct was gay and gallant,
    For he fucked all his dozens
    Of nieces and cousins,
In addition, of course, to his aunt.

There was a young man from Naragansett
Who colored his prick to enhance it.
    But the girls were afraid
    That ere they got laid
'Twould lose all its color in transit.

There was a young fellow named Price
Who dabbled in all sorts of vice.
    He had virgins and boys
    And mechanical toys,
And on Mondays... he meddled with mice!

A detective named Ellery Queen
Has olfactory powers so keen,
    He can tell in a flash
    By the scent of a gash
Who its previous tenant has been.

There was a young man from Racine
Who was weaned at the age of sixteen.
    He said, " I'll admit
    There's no milk in the tit,
But think of the fun it has been. "

The cock of a fellow named Randall
Shot sparks like a big Roman candle.
    He was much in demand,
    For the colors were grand,
But the girls found him too hot to handle.

A widow who lived in Rangoon
Hung a black-ribboned wreath on her womb,
    " To remind me, " she said,
    " Of my husband who's dead,
And of what put him into his tomb. "

There was a young man of St. James
Who indulged in the jolliest games :
    He lighted the rim
    Of his grandmother's quim,
And laughed as she pissed through the flames.

There was a young man from St. Paul's
Who read *Harper's Bazaar* and *McCall's*
    Till he grew such a passion
    For feminine fashion
That he knitted a snood for his balls.

There were three young girls in St. Thomas,
Arrived at a dance in pajamas.
    They got screwed by the drummer,
    And this went on all summer—
I'm surprised that by now they ain't mamas.

❧

There was a young lady named Smith
Whose virtue was largely a myth.
    She said, " Try as I can
    I can't find a man
Who it's fun to be virtuous with. "

❧

There once was a Monarch of Spain
Who was terribly haughty and vain.
    When women were nigh
    He'd unbutton his fly,
And screw them with signs of disdain.

❧

When the judge, with his wife having sport,
Proved suddenly two inches short,
    The good woman declined,
    And the judge had her fined
By proving contempt of the court.

" I'll admit, " said a lady named Starr,
" That a phallus is like a cigar;
    But to most common people
    A phallic church-steeple
Is stretching the matter too far. "

ॐ

There was a composer so swell
Who thought screwing to music was hell.
    Everything went fine
    Till he got out of time—
" Say, this isn't Bach, it's Ravel! "

ॐ

The mathematician Von Blecks
Devised an equation for sex,
    Having proved a good fuck
    Isn't patience or luck,
But a function of y over x.

ॐ

There was a young female named Ware
Who cut off her pubical hair.
    Then to save the men trouble
    She razored the stubble,
But none of them really did care.

WEAK SISTERS

❧

There was a young woman from Aenos
Who came to our party as Venus.
　　We told her how rude
　　’ Twas to come there quite nude,
And we brought her a leaf from the green-h’us.

❧

A girl attending Bryn Mawr
Committed a dreadful faux pas.
　　She loosened a stay
　　In her decolleté,
Exposing her je-ne-sais-quoi.

❧

A lady athletic and handsome
Got wedged in her sleeping room transom.
　　When she offered much gold
　　For release, she was told
That the view was worth more than the ransom.

There was a young girl of Oak Knoll
Who thought it exceedingly droll,
    At a masquerade ball
    Dressed in nothing at all
To back in as a Parker House roll.

❧

There was a young maid from Madras
Who had a magnificent ass;
    Not rounded and pink,
    As you probably think—
It was grey, had long ears, and ate grass.

❧

There was an old sculptor named Phidias
Whose knowledge of Art was invidious.
    He carved Aphrodite
    Without any nightie—
Which startled the purely fastidious.

❧

There's a man in the Bible portrayed
As one deeply engrossed in his trade.
    He became quite elated
    Over things he created,
Especially the women he made.

A king sadly said to his queen,
" In parts you have grown far from lean. "
   " I don't give a damn,
     You've always liked ham, "
She replied, and he gasped, " How obscene! "

I sat next to the Duchess at tea.
It was just as I feared it would be :
   Her rumblings abdominal
   Were simply phenomenal,
And everyone thought it was me!

There was a young lady of Trent
Who said that she knew what it meant
   When he asked her to dine,
   Private room, lots of wine,
She knew, oh she knew!—but she went!

There was a young lady from Wheeling
Who was out in the garden a-kneeling,
   When by some strange chance
   She got ants in her pants,
And invented Virginia reeling.

CHAMBER OF HORRORS

❧

There was a young fellow named Louvies
Who tickled his girl in the boovies,
    And as she contorted,
    He looked down and snorted,
" My prick wants to get in your movies! "

❧

There once was a gangster named Brown,
The wiliest bastard in town.
    He was caught by the G-men
    Shooting his semen
Where the cops would all slip and fall down.

❧

There was a young fellow from Eno
Who said to his girl, " Now, old Beano,
    Lift your skirt up in front,
    And enlarge your old cunt,
For the size of this organ is keen-o. "